The Essential Starter's Guide to Meta Certified Digital Marketing Associate

First Edition

Copyright © 2024 VERSAtile Reads. All rights reserved.
This material is protected by copyright, any infringement will be dealt with legal and punitive action.

Table of Contents

Meta Certified Digital Marketing Associate 7
   Introduction 7
   What is the Meta Certified Digital Marketing Associate Certification? 7
   Why Get the Meta Certified Digital Marketing Associate Certification? 7
   What Does the Meta Certification Exam Cover? 8
      Meta Technologies' Value (8%): 8
      Establishing a Business Presence (15%): 8
      Advertising Fundamentals (21%): 8
      Ad Creation and Management (46%): 8
      Reporting (10%): 8
   What Are the Benefits of Certifying? 8
   What Are the Prerequisites for Certification? 9
   What Are the Exam Fees? 9
   Navigating the Meta Certification Process 9
      Step 1: Register with Facebook Blueprint 9
      Step 2: Select Your Certification Track 9
      Step 3: Prepare for the Exam 9
      Step 4: Schedule and Take the Exam 9
      Step 5: Achieve Certification 10
   Is the Certification Worth It? 10

The Value of Meta Technologies 11
   Introduction 11
      Facebook: 11
      Messenger: 11
      Instagram: 11
      WhatsApp: 11
   Enable Connections That Matter 11
      Develop a Business Presence 11
      Sell with Shops 11
      Engage with Online Communities 11

    Gain Visibility through Ads..12

Establish Platform Presence 12

Facebook 12

    Facebook Profile vs. Page: 12

    Creating a Facebook Page: 12

Instagram 12

    Instagram Business Account: 12

    Engaging Your Audience on Instagram: 12

WhatsApp 13

    WhatsApp Business App: 13

    Best Practices: 13

Messenger 13

    Initiate Conversations: 13

The Value of Advertising 14

Case Study: Boosting Sales Efficiency with Messenger Ads 14

    Challenge: 14

    Solution: 14

    Execution: 14

    Results: 14

    Analytics and Optimization: 15

    Future Optimization: 15

    Key Takeaways: 15

Ads Policy and Data Privacy... 16

Introduction 16

The Ad Review Process 16

Causes For Ad Rejection 16

How Meta Protects User Data 17

Case Study: Setting Sail with Social Proof - Boosting Luxury Cruise Ad Recall with Authentic Customer Experiences .17

    Challenge: 17

    Strategy: 17

    Execution: 17

    Results: 17

    Analytics and Optimization: 18

| Key Takeaways: | 18 |

Start Advertising Across Meta Technologies ... 19

- Introduction ... 19
- Navigating Posts and Ads on Meta Platforms ... 19
  - Difference Between Posts and Ads: ... 19
  - Boosting a Post: ... 19
  - Promote Button: ... 19
  - Instagram Promotions: ... 19
- Meta Business Suite ... 19
- Meta Ads Manager ... 19
- Getting Started with Ads Manager ... 20
- Campaign Structure ... 20
- Case Study: From Likes to Loyalty - A Fashion Brand's Engagement Surge on Meta Platforms ... 21
  - Challenge: ... 21
  - Solution: A Multi-Faceted Approach to Rekindle the Spark ... 21
  - Results: A Social Media Makeover with Measurable Impact ... 21
  - Analytics and Optimization: ... 21

Align Your Business Goal to Your Ad Objective ... 23

- Introduction ... 23
- Access Controls Overview ... 23
  - Campaign Objective in Ads Manager ... 24
- Case Study: Gifting Growth - A British Gift Retailer Optimizes Facebook Ads for Maximum ROI ... 24
  - Challenge: Stuck in a "Present" Situation: Maximizing Return on Ad Spend ... 24
  - Solution: Thinking Beyond the Gift Basket: Introducing Brand Awareness Campaigns ... 24
  - Results: Unwrapping Success: A Multi-Objective Strategy Pays Off ... 24
  - Data Dive: Analytics and Optimization ... 25
  - Future Strategy: Building on Success ... 25
  - Key Takeaways: ... 25

Define Who Sees Your Ads ... 26

- Introduction ... 26
- Define Your Audience ... 26
  - Know Your Audience: ... 26
  - Tailor Your Audience Selection: ... 26

>   Create Audiences 26
>   New Audience 26
>   Custom Audience 26
>   Lookalike Audience 27
>   Case Study: Brushing Up on Brand Recall: An Oral Hygiene Brand Scores with Lookalike Audiences 27
>   Challenge: Forgotten Flossing? An Oral Hygiene Brand Battles Low Recall 27
>   Solution: Targeting by Lookalikes: Finding Familiar Faces in the Digital Crowd 27
>   Results: A Smile Story: Lookalike Audiences Deliver Big on Recall 27
>   Data Dive: Unpacking the Success 27
>   Key Takeaways: 27

Set Your Budget, Placement, and Schedule 29
>   Introduction 29
>   Ad Budget 29
>   Types of Budget 29
>   Budget Strategy 29
>   How Ad Pricing Works 29
>   Why Ads Don't Reach a Larger Audience 29
>   Ad Placement 30
>   Case Study: Fitness App Launch - Budget, Placement, and Schedule Optimization 30
>   Challenge: 30
>   Solution: 30

Creative Ad Formats and Strategies 33
>   Introduction 33
>   Design Ads with an Objective In Mind 33
>   Ad Formats 33
>   Best Practices for Captivating Audiences 33
>   Case Study: Cracking the Code: A Language Learning App Breaks Through the Noise with Captivating Mobile Ads ... 34
>   Challenge: Lost in Translation: A Language Learning App Needs to Be Heard 34
>   Solution: Speaking the Language of Mobile Users: Design with Intent 34
>   Results: From Applause to App Downloads: A Winning Strategy 35
>   Key Takeaways: 35

Optimize Meta Solutions 36
>   Introduction 36

    Meta Pixel and the Conversions API 36

        Add the Meta Pixel to a Website 36

    How Does Conversions API Work? 36

        Advantages of the Conversions API 36

        Standard and Custom Website Events 37

    Run A/B Tests 37

    Case Study: Metamorphosis for a Mega Retailer: How an E-commerce Giant Boosted Sales with Meta Business Suite Optimization 37

        Challenge: Stalled Sales and Fragmented Data: E-commerce Giant Seeks Conversion Magic 37

        Solution: Building a Data-Driven Bridge with Meta Business Suite 37

        Results: A Conversion Renaissance: E-commerce Giant Discovers Data-Driven Success 38

        Key Takeaways: 38

Reporting **39**

    Introduction 39

    Meta Ads Manager 39

        Default Metrics 39

        Results Metrics 39

        Cost Metrics 39

    Other Ways to Review Performance 40

        Facebook Insights: 40

        Instagram Insights: 40

    Case Study: From Scattered Data to Soaring Sales: How a Digital Marketing Agency Cracked the Code on Meta Ads Reporting 40

        Challenge: Drowning in Data, Starving for Insights 40

        Solution: Meta Ads Manager to the Rescue 41

        Results: Data-Driven Decisions, Skyrocketing Sales 41

        Key Takeaways: 41

Glossary **43**

Meta Certified Digital Marketing Associate

Introduction
Welcome to The Essential Starter's Guide to Meta Certified Digital Marketing Associate! This intensive study guide is your essential companion for preparing to ace the Meta Certified Digital Marketing Associate Certification exam. Packed with comprehensive content and strategic insights, this guide is meticulously crafted to help you master the essential concepts and skills required to excel in the field of digital marketing on Meta's platforms. Whether you're an aspiring marketing professional, a student eager to enhance your knowledge, or a seasoned marketer looking to expand your skill set, The Essential Starter's Guide to Meta Certified Digital Marketing Associate is your key to success. Let's dive in and unlock the pathway to becoming a certified digital marketing associate with Meta.

What is the Meta Certified Digital Marketing Associate Certification?
The Meta Certified Digital Marketing Associate Certification exam is designed for entry-level marketing professionals, advertising and marketing students, and interns, providing industry recognition. It caters to secondary and immediate post-secondary students, as well as career professionals seeking to enhance their skills or transition to new roles or industries.

Lasting 50 minutes, the exam comprises around 50 questions and is offered in English, German, Korean, Portuguese, Spanish, and Traditional Chinese. Successful candidates gain the competence to develop and oversee digital marketing initiatives across Meta's platforms.

Why Get the Meta Certified Digital Marketing Associate Certification?
Meta offers a wide range of certifications aimed at validating marketing professionals' skills. However, many of these certifications may be too advanced for beginners in marketing education. This is where the Meta Certified Digital Marketing Associate certification comes in, specifically tailored to assist learners in initiating or progressing their marketing careers.

Through this innovative program, participants can:

- Achieve business objectives across Facebook, Messenger, Instagram, and WhatsApp.
- Execute effective campaigns utilizing Meta's technologies.
- Generate superior-quality, innovative outputs.

Meta Certified Digital Marketing Associate

- Demonstrate proficiency in developing, overseeing, and evaluating advertisements across Meta's platforms and within the industry.
- Enhance their marketing career trajectory.

What Does the Meta Certification Exam Cover?

The Meta Certified Digital Marketing Associate certification includes five core subjects, each with corresponding sub-topics:

Meta Technologies' Value (8%):
- Recognizing Meta technologies
- Articulating the value proposition of Meta technologies for businesses

Establishing a Business Presence (15%):
- Outlining the steps to establish a business presence on Facebook, Instagram, and WhatsApp, including necessary engagement tools
- Explaining the process of customizing settings within Meta Ads Manager
- Applying creative best practices tailored for mobile experiences

Advertising Fundamentals (21%):
- Understanding the significance of advertising on Meta technologies
- Aligning business goals with ad campaign objectives
- Explaining the benefits of Meta Pixel and the Conversions API
- Clarifying the ad charging process and ad placement
- Identifying data privacy protections and common ad policies

Ad Creation and Management (46%):
- Distinguishing between boosting a Page post, promoting a post on Instagram, and creating an ad in Ads Manager
- Identifying available settings at the campaign, ad set, and ad levels
- Selecting the appropriate ad campaign objective to meet business goals
- Recognizing ad targeting capabilities
- Choosing suitable ad formats for specific scenarios
- Understanding budget and ad scheduling options
- Establishing the correlation between budget and estimated results

Reporting (10%):
- Analyzing campaign results through Meta Ads Reporting
- Evaluating campaign success metrics

What Are the Benefits of Certifying?

Certification offers a multitude of benefits that extend far beyond a mere validation of marketing skills. The Meta certification, in particular, brings a wealth of advantages to various stakeholders in the professional landscape. Some of these advantages include:
- **Enhanced Employability:** The Meta Certified Digital Marketing Associate certification serves as a powerful resume builder, showcasing candidates' proficiency in navigating major advertising platforms and boosting their appeal to potential employers.

- **Streamlined Education:** For educators, the certification offers a ready-made, self-scoring exam that saves time and enhances assessment credibility. Integrating the certification into class exams, mid-terms, or finals ensures students acquire industry-relevant skills efficiently.
- **Improved Job Placement Rates:** In workforce education, obtaining the Meta certification can significantly increase job placement rates, providing individuals with enhanced opportunities for meaningful employment and contributing to the stability of funding options.
- **Continuous Skill Enhancement:** Corporations leveraging the Meta certification empower employees to continuously enhance their job skills, fostering a culture of learning and development within the organization.
- **Mitigation of Poor Campaign Results:** By equipping employees with the necessary skills to excel in digital marketing, organizations can mitigate the risk of poor campaign outcomes, ultimately saving both time and resources.

In essence, the benefits of certifying with Meta extend far beyond individual skill validation. From enhancing employability and streamlining educational processes to driving workforce development and optimizing business outcomes, the Meta certification serves as a catalyst for growth and success across the professional landscape.

What Are the Prerequisites for Certification?

Before undertaking the Meta certification, individuals should possess the skills necessary to develop and oversee digital marketing campaigns across Meta platforms. We recommend that candidates undergo a minimum of 150 hours of instruction before attempting the exam. Proficiency at the level expected for the exam can be attained through a combination of learning and practice tests.

What Are the Exam Fees?

The pricing for Meta Certification exams typically falls within the range of USD 99 to USD 150. However, the exact cost may vary depending on the country. You will be presented with the specific cost during the checkout process.

Navigating the Meta Certification Process

Follow these steps to apply for Meta Certified Digital Marketing Associate:

Step 1: Register with Facebook Blueprint
Begin your journey by signing up for Meta Certified Digital Marketing Associate. Create an account on the website, providing the necessary details. This account serves as your central hub for learning throughout the certification process.

Step 2: Select Your Certification Track
Facebook Blueprint offers various certification tracks tailored to different skill sets and career aspirations. Choose the track that best aligns with your expertise and professional goals.

Step 3: Prepare for the Exam
Meta Certified equips you with a wealth of learning materials, including courses, videos, and resources, to aid in your exam preparation. Dive into these resources to solidify your knowledge and readiness for the certification exam.

Step 4: Schedule and Take the Exam
Conveniently schedule and take your certification exam through the website. These exams are conducted online, allowing you to choose a time that suits your schedule.

Step 5: Achieve Certification
Upon passing the exam, you'll earn the prestigious Meta Certified Digital Marketing Associate. This certification is valid for one year, after which you may opt to renew it through a recertification exam or by fulfilling additional requirements.

Is the Certification Worth It?
The value of the certification depends on your specific goals and aspirations. The courses and training modules offered are rich with valuable information, particularly beneficial for individuals new to the field. Certification badges can serve as valuable assets for freelancers aiming to expand their client base. Additionally, for those seeking employment opportunities with marketing agencies or teams, the certification can enhance credibility and competitiveness in the job market. Ultimately, whether the certification is worth it depends on how it aligns with your professional objectives and growth trajectory.

The Value of Meta Technologies

Introduction
With over 3 billion monthly users worldwide, Meta technologies have become an integral part of people's lives, facilitating connections and enabling individuals to discover what resonates with them. For businesses, harnessing the power of Meta platforms like Facebook, Messenger, Instagram, and WhatsApp presents unparalleled opportunities for growth and engagement. These platforms serve as dynamic spaces where businesses can not only stay connected with their customers but also craft compelling narratives, share updates, and showcase their products and services to vibrant communities. By leveraging Meta technologies, businesses can effectively amplify their presence, foster meaningful connections, and cultivate a thriving online presence that resonates with their audience.

Facebook:
Individuals utilize Facebook to express themselves and stay informed about global events. For businesses, Facebook serves as a vital platform for forging connections, achieving objectives, and narrating their brand stories through features like Facebook Pages and posts across various devices.

Messenger:
Messenger facilitates seamless communication between individuals and businesses, offering a convenient avenue for connection and interaction.

Instagram:
As a platform centered around photo and video sharing, Instagram inspires users to explore their interests, share passions, and foster connections within a visually engaging environment.

WhatsApp:
Businesses leverage WhatsApp to reach customers across the globe, utilizing text, voice messages, and video calls to establish connections and facilitate communication.

Enable Connections That Matter
Businesses can utilize Meta technologies to establish a robust online presence and foster meaningful connections with their audience. Meta technologies help:

Develop a Business Presence
With Facebook Pages, businesses can enhance their visibility by adding personalized information to assist customers in finding them. By sharing posts and Stories on their Facebook Pages, businesses can maintain engagement with their customer base. Tools like Meta Business Suite or Meta Creator Studio enable businesses to efficiently manage and schedule their posts, saving valuable time.

Sell with Shops
Businesses can leverage Shops as digital storefronts, offering a seamless platform to showcase their products, customize the shop's appearance, and facilitate sales transactions.

Engage with Online Communities
Businesses can enhance their presence by hosting events or participating in online groups to interact with their audience. Using Messenger, businesses can engage in direct communication with customers through sending and receiving messages.

Gain Visibility through Ads
Businesses can use Ads Manager to create advertising campaigns tailored to their business objectives. This includes creating ads, setting budgets, and choosing optimal ad placement options across Facebook, Messenger, Instagram, and Meta Audience Network.

Establish Platform Presence
Here are various ways to leverage Meta technologies for establishing a platform presence:

- Use a **Facebook Page** to establish an online presence for your business, foster community engagement, and reach out to potential customers.
- Create immersive experiences both on and off Facebook using features like **Facebook Stories**, **Reels**, **Live videos**, **Groups**, **Events**, and **Fundraisers**. Additionally, leverage Shops, appointments, and offers to sell products and services effectively.
- **Instagram Business** accounts offer valuable tools such as **Instagram Shopping**, **message management features**, and **advertising options**, helping businesses build a strong presence on the platform.
- Manage your business presence across both **Facebook** and **Instagram** seamlessly using **Meta Business Suite**.
- Enhance communication and credibility with customers using the **WhatsApp Business** app, fostering deeper relationships and facilitating effective communication.
- Use **Inbox** or **Messenger** to boost customer acquisition, streamline transactions, raise brand awareness, and deliver excellent customer service. Features like greetings, automated responses, and away messages can significantly enhance customer interactions.

Facebook
Facebook Profile vs. Page:
- **Facebook Profile:** A profile serves as your personal space on Facebook, allowing you to share details about yourself, such as your interests, photos, videos, current city, and hometown.
- **Facebook Pages:** Pages are dedicated spaces on Facebook where various entities like artists, public figures, businesses, brands, organizations, and nonprofits can engage with their fans or customers.

Creating a Facebook Page:
To set up a Facebook Business Page, it is essential to have an existing Facebook profile. Once your profile is established, you'll need the following details to create a Business Page: Your business name, business category (such as services, retail, etc.), a profile picture, cover photo, and a description outlining your business activities.

Instagram
Instagram Business Account:
To establish a Facebook Business Page, it is necessary to first have a Facebook profile in place. Once your profile is set up, you'll require the following details to create a Business Page: Your business name, business category (such as services, retail, etc.), a profile picture, cover photo, and a description outlining your business activities.

Transform your personal profile into a business account to unlock features designed to enhance your business growth. With an Instagram business account, you gain access to insights that provide valuable information about your audience engagement, track your performance metrics, access professional tools, and explore educational resources curated by Instagram.

Engaging Your Audience on Instagram:

- **Instagram Posts:** Share single or multiple photos and videos to your feed and business profile, providing valuable information about your products and services to your audience.
- **Instagram Stories:** Share short, immersive content that disappears after 24 hours, offering a glimpse into the authentic, human side of your business, including behind-the-scenes footage.
- **Reels:** Create captivating multi-clip videos up to 60 seconds long, enriched with music, audio clips, special effects, and creative tools, catering to your audience's entertainment needs.
- **Live Videos:** Stream long-form, immersive videos in fullscreen format on Instagram, ideal for bringing events online, offering exclusive content to your customers, or collaborating with other accounts. You can create or upload videos up to an hour long.

WhatsApp

WhatsApp Business App:

To get started, download the WhatsApp Business App, create an account, and establish a business profile. Once your profile setup is complete, you can begin connecting with your customers, showcase up to seven catalogs highlighting your products and services, and address inquiries throughout their shopping journey.

- **Greeting Messages:** Greeting messages allow businesses to introduce themselves to customers and can be sent automatically to individuals who initiate a conversation. These messages can include a friendly greeting, business hours, expected response times, or any other pertinent information to encourage further interaction.
- **Quick Replies:** Quick replies enable businesses to save and reuse frequently sent messages, streamlining responses to customer inquiries. These replies can also incorporate rich media elements such as GIFs, images, and videos, enhancing communication efficiency.
- **Away Messages:** Away messages automatically inform customers when a business is unavailable and indicate when they can expect a response. By setting up an away message, businesses can specify their unavailability periods, ensuring that customers receive timely notifications during these times.

Best Practices:

Implement automated away messages, instant replies, and greetings when engaging with customers directly through your WhatsApp Business Account, ensuring efficient and effective communication practices.

Messenger

Initiate Conversations:

There are numerous methods available to foster customer engagement via Messenger. Each offers a distinct approach to connecting with individuals and showcasing your business.

- **Facebook Website Plugins:** Businesses can seamlessly integrate the Messenger experience into their websites using Facebook website plugins, including Facebook Chat and Send to Messenger. These plugins facilitate direct communication between businesses and customers, enhancing the user experience.
- **M.me Links:** M.me links are unique URLs associated with your Facebook Page. When users follow or scan these links, they are directed to a Messenger conversation with your business, facilitating easy communication and interaction.
- **Click-to-Messenger Ads:** Creating ads that direct users to Messenger is an effective way to enhance brand visibility and reach potential customers across Facebook and Instagram. Ads featuring a "Send Message" button enable users to initiate conversations directly with your business, leading to lead generation, increased transactions, query resolution, and customer support.

The Value of Meta Technologies

The Value of Advertising

Perhaps you already maintain a presence on Facebook and Instagram, but aim to extend your reach and connect with new audiences. By crafting ads, you can elevate brand awareness, generate excitement surrounding your brand, and entice customers to engage with your products or services.

- **Advertising from Your Facebook Page:** There are two primary methods to advertise from your Facebook Page. You can either boost a post or create an ad using the Promote button. These actions append a Sponsored label to your post, distinguishing it as an advertisement.
- **Instagram Advertising:** Use Instagram's advertising capabilities by promoting a post directly from the platform.
- **Creating Ads with Meta Tools:** Generate ads efficiently using Meta Ads Manager, Meta Business Suite, or Meta Creator Studio. These platforms provide robust tools to streamline the ad creation process and optimize your campaign's performance.

Case Study: Boosting Sales Efficiency with Messenger Ads

Challenge:

A prominent Thai brand, known for its natural beauty products, relied heavily on social media advertising to generate conversations with potential customers. However, their existing Facebook ad strategy, focused on driving conversations, wasn't translating efficiently into sales. They needed a way to reduce their cost per purchase (CPP) and increase their return on ad spend (ROAS).

Solution:

To improve sales conversion rates, the brand implemented a strategic multi-campaign approach. They continued their existing strategy of running conversation ads on Facebook to nurture brand awareness and establish relationships with potential customers. However, they also introduced a new, dedicated Messenger ad campaign specifically designed to drive sales within the convenient and familiar Messenger platform.

Execution:

The Messenger ad campaign differed from their traditional conversation ads in several key ways:

- **Messaging and CTAs:** The ad copy and call-to-actions (CTAs) were tailored towards immediate purchase. Instead of "Learn More" or "Contact Us," the CTAs in Messenger ads were action-oriented, like "Shop Now" or "Add to Cart."
- **Rich Media Content:** The brand leveraged the visual capabilities of Messenger ads by incorporating product carousels, short product demo videos, and lifestyle imagery showcasing their products in use.
- **Seamless Buying Experience:** Importantly, the brand ensured a smooth in-app buying experience. When users clicked the CTA on a Messenger ad, they were directed to a product page within the Messenger chat window. Here, they could easily browse product details, add items to their cart, and complete their purchase entirely within Messenger.

Results:

The introduction of Messenger ads alongside their existing conversation ads resulted in significant improvements in the brand's social commerce performance:

- **15% Lower CPP:** Compared to relying solely on conversation ads, the Messenger ad campaign delivered a 15% reduction in the cost per purchase (CPP). This translates to the brand acquiring customers at a more efficient rate.
- **2x Higher Conversion Rate:** By enabling purchases directly within Messenger, the brand observed a 2x increase in conversion rates compared to their conversation ads. This suggests that users on Messenger were more likely

to complete a purchase when presented with a streamlined buying experience within the chat platform they were already familiar with.
- **Increased Customer Satisfaction:** The brand received positive customer feedback regarding the convenience of purchasing directly through Messenger. This streamlined process likely contributed to higher conversion rates and overall customer satisfaction.

Analytics and Optimization:

The brand closely monitored the performance of its Messenger ad campaign using Facebook Ads Manager. They tracked key metrics such as:

- **Click-through rate (CTR):** This measured the percentage of users who clicked on the CTA within the Messenger ad.
- **Add to cart rate:** This tracked the percentage of users who added a product to their cart after clicking on the ad.
- **Purchase completion rate:** This measured the percentage of users who completed their purchase within Messenger after adding items to their cart.

By analyzing these metrics, the brand could identify areas for improvement. For example, a low add-to-cart rate might indicate a need to adjust product descriptions or pricing within the Messenger ad experience.

Future Optimization:

Based on the success of its initial Messenger ad campaign, the brand plans to further optimize its strategy:

- **A/B Testing Ad Formats:** The brand intends to experiment with different Messenger ad formats, such as collection ads or lead generation ads, to identify the most effective approach for driving sales.
- **Tracking Customer Journey:** The brand will implement tools to track the customer journey within Messenger. This will allow them to understand how users interact with the ads, navigate the buying process, and ultimately complete their purchases. This data will be invaluable for further optimizing the buying experience within Messenger and maximizing conversions.

Key Takeaways:

- Run both brand awareness & sales-focused ads for a well-rounded social media strategy.
- Use Messenger features (CTAs, rich media, in-app purchases) to drive sales within the familiar platform.
- Use data (CTR, add-to-cart rate) to improve your Messenger ad experience for better results.
- Experiment with ad formats to see what works best for your audience.

Note: Businesses have the opportunity to leverage Meta technologies, including Facebook, Messenger, Instagram, and WhatsApp, as powerful tools for business growth, customer engagement, storytelling, and community sharing.

Ads Policy and Data Privacy

Introduction
In this section, we outline Meta's rigorous Ad Review Process and its commitment to user data privacy. From scrutinizing ads for compliance with advertising policies to safeguarding user information through features like Privacy Checkup, Meta prioritizes maintaining a secure and compliant advertising ecosystem. We also highlight reasons for ad rejection and measures to empower users with control over their shared content and account security.

The Ad Review Process
Here's how the ad review process works:

- **Step #1:** The system scrutinizes various elements of your ad, including images, video, corresponding thumbnail, text, targeting, and positioning, in accordance with Meta Advertising Policy.
- **Step #2:** The ad's landing page undergoes evaluation for both content and functionality, ensuring alignment with the product or service promoted in the ad.
- **Step #3:** Pre- and post-publication, the system monitors the ad's performance, especially in cases where individuals hide, block, or express negative feedback about the ad.

Typically, ad reviews are completed within 24 hours, although occasionally, it may take longer. Following the review, you will receive a notification regarding the approval status of your ad.

Causes For Ad Rejection
Reasons for ad rejection include:

- **Selling illegal products or services:** Ads must refrain from endorsing, facilitating, or promoting illegal products, services, or activities.
- **Landing Pages:** Ads should not direct users to landing pages that are dysfunctional, offer unexpected or disruptive experiences, or fail to align with the advertised product or service.
- **Personal Attributes:** Ads should avoid containing content that directly or indirectly asserts or implies personal attributes, such as race, ethnicity, religion, beliefs, age, gender identity, disability, physical or mental health (including medical condition), financial vulnerability, voting status, trade union membership, criminal record, or name.
- **Discriminatory Practices:** Ads must not engage in or endorse discrimination against individuals based on personal attributes, such as race, ethnicity, color, national origin, religion, age, gender, family status, disability, or medical or genetic condition.
- **Tobacco and Related Products:** Ads must refrain from promoting the sale or use of tobacco products and related paraphernalia.
- **Weapons, Ammunition, or Explosives:** Ads should not promote the sale or use of weapons, ammunition, or explosives.
- **Adult Content, Products, or Services:** Ads must not display images or videos of an explicit nature.

How Meta Protects User Data

Meta offers features such as Privacy Checkup to empower users with control over their shared content, audience visibility, displayed content, and communication preferences.

Through the Privacy Checkup tool, users can activate two-factor authentication and login alerts. Enabling alerts allows Meta to notify users if their account is accessed from an unrecognized location.

Case Study: Setting Sail with Social Proof - Boosting Luxury Cruise Ad Recall with Authentic Customer Experiences

Challenge:
In an increasingly crowded travel market, a luxury cruise operator needed to cut through the noise and make a lasting impression on potential high-end customers. Their primary goal was to significantly improve ad recall and brand awareness for their luxury cruises.

Strategy:
The strategy capitalized on the power of social media storytelling to showcase the essence of the luxury cruise experience. Facebook and Instagram, with their vast user base and advanced targeting capabilities, were identified as the ideal platforms to reach their target audience.

Execution:
- **Vivid Destination Storytelling:** Breathtaking, high-resolution video ads took center stage. These weren't simply generic travel montages; they were meticulously crafted to showcase the unique features and immersive experiences offered by the cruise line. Imagine captivating scenes: crystal-clear waters lapping at pristine beaches in the Caribbean, followed by a panoramic view of a historic European city at sunset, all set to a soundtrack that evokes a sense of relaxation and adventure.
- **Authentic Customer Testimonials:** To move beyond aspirational imagery and forge a deeper connection, the video ads incorporated real customer testimonials. Satisfied passengers from diverse backgrounds shared their personal experiences, highlighting the onboard amenities, exceptional service, and unforgettable destinations. Seeing real people genuinely enjoying themselves on the cruises lent credibility and authenticity to the campaign, fostering trust with potential customers.
- **Targeted Audience Reach:** Leveraging Facebook and Instagram's advanced targeting tools, the campaign ensured the ads reached the most relevant audience segments. By factoring in demographics, interests (luxury travel, fine dining, cultural exploration), and past travel behavior, the cruise operator ensured their message resonated with those most likely to be interested in a luxury cruise adventure.

Results:
The campaign exceeded expectations, achieving impressive results:

- **Soaring Ad Recall:** The campaign delivered a significant 11-point increase in ad recall among the target audience. This means that after viewing the ads, potential customers were much more likely to remember the cruise operator when considering their next vacation.
- **Engagement and Emotional Connection:** The use of real customer testimonials proved to be a powerful strategy. Viewers engaged with the ads at a higher rate compared to previous campaigns that relied solely on generic visuals. The emotional connection fostered by genuine customer experiences resonated with potential customers, whetting their appetite for a similar luxurious adventure.
- **Website Traffic & Lead Generation:** The compelling storytelling and targeted approach resulted in a substantial increase in website traffic. Engaged viewers were more likely to visit the cruise operator's website to explore

Ads Policy and Data Privacy

specific itineraries, pricing, and special offers. This translated into a significant rise in qualified leads, indicating a strong interest in booking a cruise.

Analytics and Optimization:

Throughout the campaign, the cruise operator's marketing team closely monitored key performance indicators (KPIs) using Facebook Ads Manager and Instagram Insights. These metrics included:

- **Ad recall lift:** Measured through brand lift studies conducted after the campaign concluded.
- **View rates and completion rates:** Indicated how many viewers saw the ad and how many watched it all the way through.
- **Click-Through Rates (CTR):** Tracked the percentage of viewers who clicked on the ad to visit the cruise operator's website.
- **Website traffic and lead generation:** Measured the impact of the campaign on overall website traffic and the number of qualified leads generated.

By analyzing this data, the marketing team could identify areas for improvement and optimize the campaign in real-time. For example, if a particular customer testimonial resonated strongly with viewers, they could increase the ad spend for that video to reach a wider audience.

Key Takeaways:

- Leverage Facebook & Instagram for targeted video ads showcasing the essence of your luxury experience.
- Feature real customer testimonials to build trust and credibility with potential high-end customers.
- Utilize advanced targeting tools to ensure your message resonates with those most likely to convert.
- Track key metrics (ad recall, view rates, CTR) and optimize the campaign for maximum impact.

Notes:
- Expand your Audience Reach and Foster New Customer Connections with Meta.
- Meta equips users with tools such as Privacy Checkup, two-factor authentication, and login alerts to regulate their shared content and audience accessibility, along with security options to safeguard their accounts.
- Ads on Meta undergo thorough review to ensure compliance with our policies regarding permissible ad content types.

Start Advertising Across Meta Technologies

Introduction
Engaging with your target audience on Meta Platforms involves a strategic mix of organic content and paid advertising. This section will equip you with the knowledge to navigate both posts and ads effectively. We'll explore the key differences between the two, delve into boosting options and the Promote button, and uncover the functionalities of Meta Business Suite and Meta Ads Manager.

Navigating Posts and Ads on Meta Platforms

Difference Between Posts and Ads:
Businesses leverage Facebook Pages to share content about their products and services, fostering their online brand presence. This content is showcased to their page followers. However, to reach individuals unfamiliar with their offerings, businesses can opt to advertise on Meta technologies. These advertisements are designated with a Sponsored label.

Boosting a Post:
Boosted posts are advertisements created from existing posts on a Facebook Page or Instagram account. Boosting a post aims to enhance engagement and garner more messages, leads, or calls. It also facilitates reaching new potential followers or customers who exhibit interest in the business but aren't currently following them.

Promote Button:
Alternatively, businesses can create new advertisements directly from their Facebook Page using the Promote button without relying on existing posts. Various ad types and settings are available to cater to each business's unique objectives.

Instagram Promotions:
Businesses can promote existing posts or Stories on Instagram, effectively transforming them into ads to expand their reach and engagement on the platform.

Meta Business Suite
Meta Business Suite enables centralized management of all connected accounts across Facebook and Instagram. With this tool, you can:

- Create, schedule, and oversee posts and Stories across your Facebook Page and Instagram account.
- Seamlessly engage with customers by responding to all messages in a unified interface.
- Gain valuable insights into audience interactions with posts, Stories, and ads.
- Access Meta Business Suite conveniently through both desktop and mobile applications.

Meta Ads Manager
Meta Ads Manager serves as the central hub for managing ad campaigns across various platforms such as Facebook, Messenger, Instagram, and WhatsApp. It provides a comprehensive toolkit for creating ads, controlling their scheduling and placement, and monitoring campaign performance. Ads Manager is accessible via desktop or mobile application.

Why is Ads Manager such a useful tool?

- **Streamlined Ad Creation:** Ads Manager allows you to efficiently create and oversee multiple ads simultaneously. Within the platform, you can adjust settings like target audience, budget, and ad placements, as well as generate duplicates of your ads.
- **Effective Ad Management:** You can easily monitor data and assess the performance of your ads, accessing real-time insights and scheduling reports to stay informed about campaign progress.
- **Insightful Performance Evaluation:** By analyzing results at both the account and campaign levels, you gain a comprehensive view of your campaigns' effectiveness. Additionally, you can apply breakdowns to focus on specific metrics of interest and generate or schedule ad reports accordingly.

Furthermore, while every personal Facebook account automatically includes an associated Ads Manager account, advertisers require authorization from a Facebook Page or Instagram Business Account to create ads.

Getting Started with Ads Manager

1. Ensure you have a Facebook Page. Upon creating a Page, you'll automatically gain access to an Ads Manager account.
2. Once inside Ads Manager, navigate to the ad account settings tab to verify account details, including:
   1. Currency
   2. Time zone
   3. Spending limit
   4. Payment method

To initiate ad campaigns, follow these steps:

1. Access your Ads Manager to review your automatically assigned account ID number, currency, and time zone. You have the option to modify your currency and time zone, though doing so will result in the creation of a new Ads Manager account.
2. Within Business Info, specify your advertising purpose, business name, and address. This information is essential for legal compliance, considering potential advertising restrictions in your area.
3. Configure your payment method and establish an account spending limit.

Campaign Structure

In Ads Manager, the campaign framework comprises three tiers:

Start Advertising Across Meta Technologies

Please note that the campaign levels and their components may be accessible in a different order than depicted in the chart. Nonetheless, the illustrated sequence aims to provide clarity on how all elements are interconnected.

Case Study: From Likes to Loyalty - A Fashion Brand's Engagement Surge on Meta Platforms

Challenge:
A fashion brand, struggling to connect with its target audience despite a sizeable following on Facebook and Instagram, needed a strategy to reignite engagement and convert followers into loyal customers. Their social media presence, while visually appealing, lacked the spark to foster meaningful interactions or drive sales.

Solution: A Multi-Faceted Approach to Rekindle the Spark
The brand embarked on a comprehensive strategy focused on three key pillars:

- **Content that Captivates:** Static product shots were replaced with visually engaging and relatable posts. Eye-catching product stories showcased new arrivals in action. Behind-the-scenes glimpses offered a peek into the creative process, humanizing the brand. User-generated content (UGC) played a starring role, featuring real customers rocking the brand's latest looks.
- **Targeted Ads that Convert:** Leveraging Meta Ads Manager, the brand launched targeted ad campaigns that put their products directly in front of their ideal customer. These campaigns utilized a strategic mix of formats: eye-catching image ads showcasing statement pieces, short and trendy video ads highlighting key features of new arrivals, and dynamic carousel ads offering a glimpse of a curated collection.
- **Interactive Features that Foster Community:** The brand understood the power of connection. They began incorporating interactive features into their social media strategy. Polls gauged audience preferences on upcoming trends, while quizzes helped followers discover their personal style aesthetic. Instagram Stories became a playground for engagement, with interactive stickers like "Ask Me Anything" sessions with stylists and "Poll" stickers to determine the most coveted pieces from a new collection. This interactive approach fostered a sense of community and encouraged followers to not just view content but actively participate in the brand conversation.

Results: A Social Media Makeover with Measurable Impact
The brand's strategic shift yielded impressive outcomes:

- **Engagement Soared:** Likes, comments, and shares saw a significant increase across both Facebook and Instagram. The brand's content resonated with its audience, sparking conversations and fostering a sense of community.
- **Brand Awareness Amplified:** Targeted ad campaigns delivered the brand's message directly to their ideal customer base. This translated to a noticeable rise in brand awareness, with the brand appearing on the radar of potential customers who might have previously overlooked it.
- **Sales Conversion Climbed:** The most crucial metric - sales - saw a positive uptick. Driving traffic to their website with compelling product showcases in ads, coupled with increased engagement and brand loyalty, led to a measurable surge in online sales and conversions.

Analytics and Optimization:
The brand's marketing team became data-driven decision-makers. They closely monitored key performance indicators (KPIs) using Facebook Ads Manager and Instagram Insights.

These metrics included:

Start Advertising Across Meta Technologies

- **Engagement rate:** Measured by the average number of likes, comments, and shares per post, this KPI gave them a clear picture of how well their content resonated with their audience.
- **Click-through rate (CTR):** This tracked the percentage of viewers who clicked on their ads to visit the brand's website. A high CTR indicated that their ad creative and targeting were effective.
- **Website traffic and conversion rate:** This measured the impact of their social media strategy on overall website traffic and the number of visitors who completed a purchase.

By analyzing this data, the brand could identify areas for improvement and optimize its social media strategy in real time. For example, if a particular UGC post featuring a specific style influencer generated high engagement, they could partner with that influencer for a future campaign.

Key Takeaways:
- Feature user-generated content, behind-the-scenes glimpses, and style inspiration.
- Reach ideal customers with a mix of image, video, and carousel ads on social media platforms.
- Foster community with polls, quizzes, and Instagram Stories to encourage audience participation.
- Track key metrics (engagement rate, CTR, traffic) and adapt your social media strategy for success.

Notes:
- Meta ads enable businesses to expand their customer base and are identified with a Sponsored label.
- Enhance the visibility of your content by boosting a Page post, promoting an Instagram post, or creating an ad directly from your Page using the promote button.
- Employ an Ads Manager for the seamless creation and supervision of synchronized campaigns.
- Campaigns are structured into three levels: campaign, ad set, and ads.

Align Your Business Goal to Your Ad Objective

Introduction
Crafting successful ad campaigns on Meta Platforms starts with a clear understanding of your business goals. This section will delve into the concept of Campaign Objectives within Ads Manager, explaining how they guide Meta's delivery of your ads and ultimately influence campaign effectiveness.

Access Controls Overview
Ads Manager provides a diverse range of campaign objectives for your selection. Prior to choosing your campaign objective, it's imperative to delineate your business goal to ensure alignment with the corresponding objective. Selecting the appropriate objective is paramount as it dictates Meta's approach to delivering your ads. Presently, they offer six objectives covering three stages of the consumer journey:

- **Awareness:** These objectives aim to stimulate interest in a business's products or services. Enhancing brand awareness revolves around communicating the unique value proposition of a business.
- **Consideration:** These objectives prompt individuals to contemplate a business' offerings and seek further information about them.
- **Conversion:** These objectives motivate individuals interested in a business to undertake a specific action, such as making a purchase.

Customer journey stage	Objectives	Goals	Good for...
Awareness	Awareness	Show your ads to people who are most likely to remember them.	• Reach • Brand awareness • Video views
Consideration	Traffic	Send people to a destination, like your website, app or Facebook event.	• Link clicks • Landing page views
	Engagement	Get more video views, post engagement, Page likes or event responses.	• Messages • Video views • Post engagement
	Leads	Collect leads for your business or brand.	• Instant forms • Messages • Calls • Sign-ups
Conversion	App promotion	Find new people to install your app and continue using it.	• App installs • App events
	Sales	Find people likely to purchase your product or service.	• Conversions • Catalog sales • Messages

Align Your Business Goal to Your Ad Objective

Campaign Objective in Ads Manager

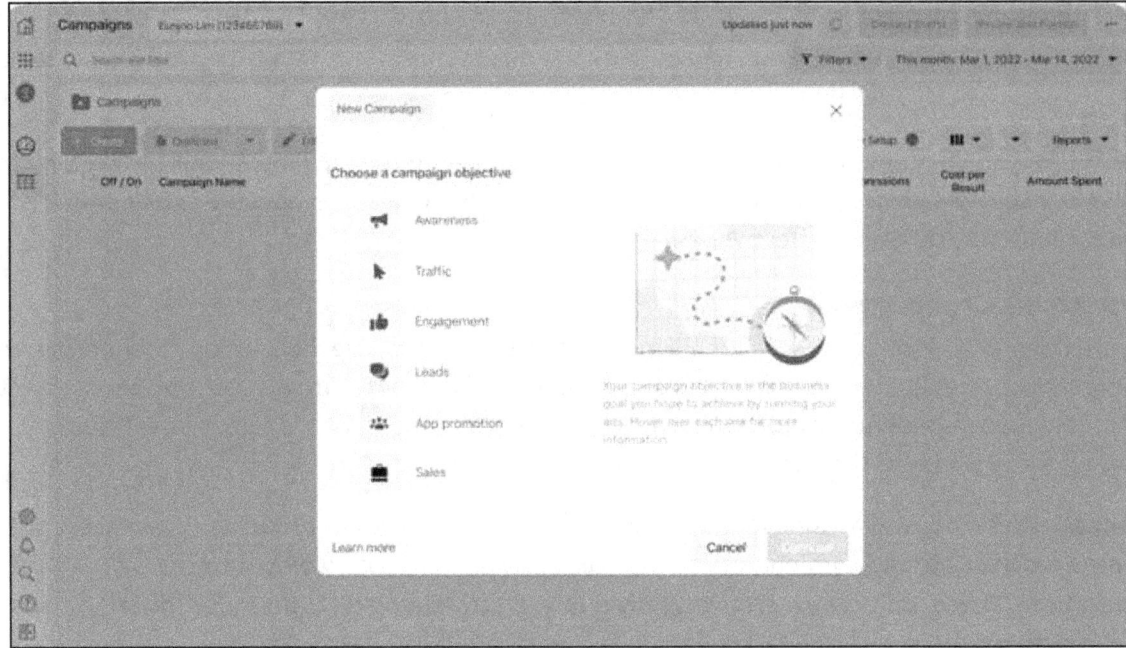

Case Study: Gifting Growth - A British Gift Retailer Optimizes Facebook Ads for Maximum ROI

Challenge: Stuck in a "Present" Situation: Maximizing Return on Ad Spend
A British gift retailer, brimming with unique treasures, found itself in a familiar predicament. Their Facebook advertising strategy, while successful in driving sales, wasn't stretching its budget as far as they'd hoped. Their primary focus on conversion-oriented ads meant they weren't capturing the full potential of their target audience. The challenge? To elevate their return on ad spend (ROAS) and unlock new avenues for growth.

Solution: Thinking Beyond the Gift Basket: Introducing Brand Awareness Campaigns
The retailer knew they needed to expand their approach. They implemented a multi-objective strategy, strategically incorporating brand awareness campaigns alongside their existing sales-focused Facebook ads. This wasn't about abandoning their tried-and-true methods; it was about adding a new layer to their advertising strategy.

The brand awareness campaigns focused on broader storytelling. Eye-catching video ads showcased the heartwarming emotions associated with gift-giving, featuring families celebrating birthdays, friends exchanging thoughtful tokens, and couples marking special occasions. Interactive quizzes helped users discover their ideal gift based on personality and occasion. Compelling blog posts, shared directly on Facebook, offered gift-giving inspiration and trend reports.

Results: Unwrapping Success: A Multi-Objective Strategy Pays Off
The multi-objective approach proved to be a gift that kept on giving:

- **Soaring ROAS:** The brand awareness campaigns, while not directly driving immediate sales, likely contributed to increased brand recognition. This resulted in a significant 56% uplift in incremental ROAS from their existing sales-focused ads. In simpler terms, for every pound spent, they were seeing a much higher return in overall sales.

Data Dive: Analytics and Optimization
The retailer prioritized data-driven decision-making. They closely monitored key performance indicators (KPIs) within Facebook Ads Manager:

- **Reach and impressions:** Measured the number of unique users who saw their brand awareness ads.
- **Engagement rate:** Tracked how well their brand awareness content resonated with viewers, measured by likes, comments, and shares.
- **Click-through rate (CTR):** Indicated the percentage of viewers who clicked through from the brand awareness ads to visit the retailer's website, potentially for future purchases.
- **Website traffic and conversion rate:** Measured the overall impact of the campaign on website traffic and the number of visitors who ultimately made a purchase.

By analyzing this data, the retailer could identify areas for improvement and optimize their campaigns on an ongoing basis. For example, a brand awareness video ad featuring a particular gift category (think "unique gifts for men") that generated a high CTR might lead them to create a targeted sales campaign specifically focused on those products.

Future Strategy: Building on Success
Encouraged by the positive results, the retailer plans to further refine its strategy:

- **Customer Journey Tracking:** Implementing robust website tracking tools will allow them to map the customer journey, from initial brand awareness exposure to final purchase. This data will be invaluable for creating even more targeted and personalized ad campaigns in the future.
- **Testing Reach Ad Formats:** The brand plans to experiment with different ad formats within its brand awareness campaigns. This might include exploring carousels showcasing a variety of gift ideas or leveraging Facebook Stories to offer behind-the-scenes glimpses into their charming store and unique products.

Key Takeaways:
- Combine brand awareness campaigns with conversion-focused ads for a well-rounded Facebook Ads approach.
- Invest in brand awareness campaigns to build recognition and trust, leading to higher return on ad spend (ROAS) in the long run.
- Track key metrics (reach, engagement, CTR) to analyze campaign effectiveness and optimize ad creatives and targeting.
- Understand how users interact with your brand awareness and sales ads to personalize future campaigns.
- Experiment with different ad formats (video, carousels, Stories) to discover the most engaging tactics for brand awareness goals.

Notes:
- Consider your business objective carefully when crafting your ad campaign, ensuring alignment with the most suitable ad objective.
- The ad objectives are divided into three main categories: Awareness, Consideration, and Conversion.
- In total, there are six ad objectives available: Awareness, Traffic, Engagement, App Promotions, Leads, and Sales.

Define Who Sees Your Ads

Introduction
The success of any ad campaign hinges on reaching the right people. This section empowers you to take control by defining who sees your ads on Meta Platforms. We'll dive into the characteristics of your ideal customer and explore the powerful tools within Meta Ads Manager that help you build a targeted audience for maximum impact.

Define Your Audience
Before crafting your ad, it's crucial to identify your ideal customer. This section will guide you through defining your target audience and leveraging Meta Ads Manager to reach them effectively.

Know Your Audience:
- Uncover their needs, characteristics, and motivations. Understanding what drives your ideal customer is key to shaping a compelling ad.
- Consider demographics, interests, and behaviors. These factors help you create a detailed profile of who you want to reach.

Tailor Your Audience Selection:
Meta Ads Manager offers several audience-building options:

- **New Audiences:** Define demographics (age, location), interests (hobbies, brands), and behaviors (online activity) to reach a broad or specific audience.
- **Custom Audiences:** Reconnect with existing customers who have interacted with your website, app, or social media pages. Upload your email list or customer data to target them across Meta platforms.
- **Lookalike Audiences:** Expand your reach by targeting new people who share similar characteristics with your existing customers. This is a powerful way to find potential customers likely to resonate with your ad.

By understanding your audience and utilizing these tools, you can ensure your ads are seen by the right people, maximizing your campaign's impact.

Create Audiences
Audiences are generated and managed within the ad set framework.

New Audience
The default audience for an ad set in Ads Manager is the new audience. To define a new audience, you can specify attributes like location, demographics, interests, behaviors, and connections.

Custom Audience
Businesses have the option to utilize diverse data sources for forming Custom Audiences. To create a Custom Audience, navigate to "Create new audience." Then, choose "Create new" from the dropdown menu, opening a list. From there, opt for "Custom Audience" in the dropdown menu and select your preferred data source.

Lookalike Audience
To craft a lookalike audience, initiate the same initial steps as you would for generating a Custom Audience. Select "Create new" and opt for "Lookalike Audience" from the dropdown menu.

Case Study: Brushing Up on Brand Recall: An Oral Hygiene Brand Scores with Lookalike Audiences

Challenge: Forgotten Flossing? An Oral Hygiene Brand Battles Low Recall
An oral hygiene brand, known for its innovative line of electric toothbrushes and whitening rinses, faced a disheartening reality. Despite running a comprehensive Facebook and Instagram ad campaign featuring eye-catching visuals and informative product descriptions, their brand recall metrics were abysmal. In simpler terms, people just weren't remembering their ads. This translated into a missed opportunity to connect with potential customers and convert interest into sales.

Solution: Targeting by Lookalikes: Finding Familiar Faces in the Digital Crowd
The oral hygiene brand knew they needed a more strategic approach. They decided to leverage Facebook's advanced targeting capabilities by incorporating **lookalike audiences**. This powerful feature allowed them to target users who shared similar characteristics and online behaviors with their existing high-value customers.

Here's how it worked: The brand utilized its existing customer data (think demographics, purchase history, website behavior) to create a "seed audience" of their most engaged customers. Facebook then analyzed this data and identified new users across the platform who mirrored these characteristics. Voila! A targeted audience brimming with potential.

But targeting alone wasn't enough. To truly capture attention, the brand needed engaging ad creative. They opted for compelling video ads that showcased the benefits of their products in an actionable way. Think before-and-after smiles, time-lapse teeth whitening transformations, and authentic user testimonials from individuals raving about the positive impact the brand's products had on their oral health routines.

Results: A Smile Story: Lookalike Audiences Deliver Big on Recall
The implementation of the lookalike audience video ad campaign proved to be a game-changer:

- **Soaring Ad Recall:** The brand witnessed a remarkable 6X increase in ad recall. This meant that people weren't just seeing the ads; they were remembering them. The combination of targeted lookalike audiences and engaging video content effectively cut through the digital noise and left a lasting impression on the target audience.

Data Dive: Unpacking the Success
Beyond the headline result, the brand delved deeper into the data to understand the "why" behind their success:

- **Engagement Metrics:** Lookalike audiences were more likely to click on the video ads, compared to the broader audience targeted in their previous campaign. This indicated a higher level of interest and receptiveness to the brand's message.
- **Website Traffic & Conversion Rates:** The increased ad recall translated into a significant rise in website traffic. More importantly, those website visitors were more likely to convert into paying customers, showcasing the effectiveness of the lookalike audience approach in driving sales.

Key Takeaways:
- Target users similar to high-value customers for better ad reception.

Define Who Sees Your Ads

- Capture attention and showcase product benefits for improved brand recall.
- Targeted ads lead to viewers actively engaging with your content.
- Effective campaigns drive qualified traffic and sales.
- Targeted messaging builds brand recognition and fosters customer loyalty.

Notes:
- Understand the requirements, attributes, and drives of your business's optimal audience to refine your target audience during ad creation.
- Use Custom Audiences to engage with customers already connected to your business.
- Employ lookalike audiences to connect with individuals sharing similarities with your existing customer base.

Set Your Budget, Placement, and Schedule

Introduction
Creating a winning ad campaign goes beyond just the creative. This section empowers you to take control of three crucial elements – Budget, Placement, and Schedule – that significantly influence your ad's success. We'll explore different budget types and strategies, delve into ad placement options, and guide you through scheduling your campaign for optimal reach. By strategically setting these parameters, you'll ensure your ad reaches the right audience at the right time, maximizing its impact and return on investment.

Ad Budget

Types of Budget
Two budget choices are available to optimize your ad expenditure:

- **Daily Budget:** The average sum allocated for an ad set or campaign on a daily basis.
- **Lifetime Budget:** The total amount designated for an ad set or campaign throughout its entire duration.

Opting for a lifetime budget empowers you to enhance outcomes while maintaining overall expenses at a minimum. Conversely, a daily budget limits Meta technologies from fully exploring opportunities over the campaign's lifetime.

Budget Strategy
- The Campaign Budget Optimization feature, now known as the Advantage campaign budget, offers an option at the campaign level to establish a single overarching budget instead of allocating budgets to individual ad sets. This optimization allows for more flexibility, directing more funds towards ad sets with promising opportunities while allocating less to underperforming ones.
- Individual ad set budgets provide the capability to assign a specific budget to each ad set, offering greater control over budget allocation.
- Use tools such as estimated audience size and estimated daily results to assess potential outcomes based on a particular budget and adjust as necessary.

How Ad Pricing Works
Depending on the selected ad objective, you will incur charges based on impressions, clicks, or actions.

- **Impressions:** Charges are applied for every 1,000 impressions received on a campaign, denoted as cost per 1,000 impressions (CPM).
- **Clicks:** Charges are incurred for each click on an ad, referred to as cost per click (CPC).
- **Actions:** Charges are applied each time a user completes the desired action, termed cost per action (CPA).

Why Ads Don't Reach a Larger Audience
There are multiple factors contributing to low ad reach:

- Inadequate ad set budget, impacting estimated daily reach and overall ad performance.
- Narrow or small audience selection.
- Misalignment with your target audience.

Set Your Budget, Placement, and Schedule

Estimated daily results for your ads may fluctuate depending on the chosen campaign objective.

Ad Placement

- When crafting an ad through Ads Manager, you have the option to specify its appearance across Facebook, Messenger, Instagram, and the Meta Audience Network. The Audience Network extends ad campaigns to third-party apps, broadening their reach.
- Meta recommends utilizing Advantage+ placements for optimal budget efficiency, as it directs ad content to achieve campaign goals at the lowest feasible cost.
- Alternatively, with manual placements, you can tailor where your ad appears across various Meta platforms. Employing multiple placements enhances audience reach and maximizes budget utilization.
- Additionally, combining the Advantage campaign budget and Advantage+ placements offers a highly adaptable bid strategy with substantial scalability. This approach adjusts bids dynamically to minimize cost per result while adhering to your budget constraints, ensuring optimal results even amidst fluctuating costs.
- Ad placement selection occurs at the ad set level within Ads Manager.

Surface	Placement option
feeds	Facebook Feed, Instagram feed, Facebook Marketplace, Facebook video feeds, Facebook right column, Instagram Explore, Instagram Shop, Messenger Inbox
Stories	Facebook Stories, Messenger Stories, Instagram Stories, Instagram Reels, Facebook Reels
In-Stream videos	Facebook In-stream videos
search	Facebook search results
messages	Messenger sponsored messages
in-ad article	Facebook Instant Articles
apps and sites	Audience Network native, banner and interstitial, Audience Network rewarded videos, Audience Network In-stream videos

Case Study: Fitness App Launch - Budget, Placement, and Schedule Optimization

Challenge:

A fitness app offering personalized workout plans needed a successful launch with a limited marketing budget. The goal was to maximize app downloads and achieve a positive return on investment (ROI).

Solution:

Budget and Strategy:

- **Lifetime Budget with Advantage Bidding:** A total budget of $50,000 was allocated, with daily spend fluctuating based on performance, allowing the platform's algorithms to optimize spending throughout the 2-month campaign.

Set Your Budget, Placement, and Schedule

- **Targeted Ad Sets:** Separate ad sets were created with individual budgets for:
    - Young professionals (urban areas)
    - Stay-at-home parents (suburban areas)
    - Fitness enthuslasts
    - Weight loss seekers (interested in healthy eating)
- **Estimated Results:** Using the platform's estimated daily results tool, the app anticipated 200-250 downloads per day.

Ad Pricing and Campaign Objective:

- **Cost per Action (CPA):** A CPA goal of $3.00 per download ensured the app was only charged for successful downloads, not just ad impressions.

Addressing Limited Reach:

- **Expanded Audience Targeting:** Beyond demographics, the target audience included users with fitness interests, those who used similar apps, and people who interacted with fitness content on the platform.

- **Estimated Daily Reach:** A target of 250,000 daily impressions was set, with adjustments made as needed to maintain this goal.

Deciding on Ad Placement:

- **Advantage+ placements:** This maximized budget efficiency by reaching the target audience across various platforms within the network.
- **Manual placements:** Ads were also placed in specific fitness apps and relevant Facebook groups for a more targeted reach.

Utilizing Schedule Flexibility:

- **Strategic Campaign Duration:** The launch capitalized on the "New Year's resolution" season, running for 8 weeks from mid-November to mid-January.
- **Ad Set Scheduling:** User behavior data-informed adjustments to ad set scheduling. For example, young professionals responded best to lunch break ads (12-1 pm), while stay-at-home parents preferred evening ads (7-9 pm).

Results:

The campaign exceeded expectations within budget constraints:

- **App Downloads:** 18,500 new users were acquired at a cost of $2.80 per download (under the $3.00 CPA goal).
- **Reach:** An average of 280,000 people were reached daily.
- **Engagement:** The click-through rate (CTR) of 1.2% surpassed industry benchmarks, indicating strong ad creative that resonated with the target audience.

Key Takeaways:

This case study demonstrates the effectiveness of strategic campaign management. By utilizing:

- A Lifetime Budget with Advantage Bidding
- Tailored Ad Sets with demographics and budgets
- Estimated daily reach and results tools

Set Your Budget, Placement, and Schedule

- A combination of Advantage+ and manual placements
- User behavior-based ad scheduling

> **Notes:**
> - You have the option to choose between a daily budget or a lifetime budget. For efficient allocation of ad spend across your ad sets, consider utilizing the Advantage campaign budget.
> - Ads created via Ads Manager have the potential to appear across various platforms, including Facebook, Messenger, Instagram, and the Audience Network.
> - Use estimated audience size and estimated daily results tools to assess performance and make necessary adjustments.
> - Employ tools like Advantage campaign budget and Advantage+ placements concurrently to maintain the profitability and effectiveness of your ad campaign in the long run.

Creative Ad Formats and Strategies

Introduction
Creating captivating ads is an art form, and Meta Ads Manager provides the tools you need to be a master. This section delves into the essential ingredients for crafting impactful ads – understanding your objective, selecting the perfect format, and following best practices for mobile audiences.

Design Ads with an Objective In Mind
When crafting your ad, it's crucial to choose photos or videos aligned with your objective to encourage the desired response from your audience. Here are three questions to ponder during the design process:

1. What product or service am I promoting, and how will it contribute to achieving my business objectives throughout the ad campaign duration?
2. Which types of visuals, including images, videos, and concise text, can effectively support my business goals while complying with the available ad formats?
3. Who is the intended audience for my ads, and how can the creative content captivate and resonate with the specific audience I'm targeting?

Ad Formats
The right format can make all the difference in captivating your audience. This section dives into the diverse ad formats available in Meta Ads Manager, allowing you to tailor your message for maximum impact.

- **Classic Image and Video Ads:** Grab attention with powerful visuals. Images showcase products, services, or brand identity, while videos offer a more immersive storytelling experience.
- **Carousel Ads:** Showcase a variety of products, features, or benefits within a single ad. With up to 10 images or videos, each linked to its own URL, carousel ads provide a dynamic and informative experience for viewers.
- **Slideshow Ads:** Create high-quality, engaging mini-videos using images, text, and sound. Slideshow ads are a cost-effective way to tell a compelling story and capture your audience's attention.
- **Collection Ads:** Seamlessly combine the power of images or videos with detailed product information. This format is ideal for showcasing product lines or collections, allowing viewers to easily explore different options.
- **Immersive Instant Experiences:** Take your audience beyond the ad with a full-screen, interactive experience. Instant Experiences let you showcase your brand in a captivating way, driving deeper engagement and brand awareness.

By understanding these ad format options, you can choose the best fit to deliver your message effectively and resonate with your target audience.

Best Practices for Captivating Audiences
When it comes to mobile advertising, every second counts. Here are some best practices to follow for mobile-friendly creatives:

- **Hook Them Fast:** Deliver your key message or product within the first 3 seconds. This prime window is crucial for capturing attention and ensuring your ad is remembered.

Creative Ad Formats and Strategies

- **Sound Off Success:** Many viewers watch mobile videos with the sound off. Design your ads to be impactful even without audio. Utilize clear visuals, captions, and text overlays to effectively communicate your message.
- **Mobile-First Mindset:** Ensure your ad format is optimized for mobile viewing. Double-check aspect ratios to guarantee your image or video displays correctly. Prioritize clear visuals and legible text for optimal impact on smaller screens.
- **Clarity is Key:** Craft concise captions with a clear call to action (CTA). Use these captions to tell your brand story and guide viewers toward the desired action.
- **Cohesive Brand Identity:** Maintaining a consistent look and feel across your ads reinforces brand recognition. Viewers should instantly identify your brand, regardless of where they encounter your ad.
- **Plan Your Content:** Develop a content calendar to strategize your social media presence. This includes planning what content to share, when to post, and on which platforms.
- **Harness the Power of Tags:** Expand your reach and discoverability by incorporating relevant hashtags, location tags, and mentions within your posts. This helps potential customers find your content more easily.

By adhering to these best practices, you can create mobile-optimized ads that effectively capture attention, tell your brand story, and drive results.

Case Study: Cracking the Code: A Language Learning App Breaks Through the Noise with Captivating Mobile Ads

Challenge: Lost in Translation: A Language Learning App Needs to Be Heard

Imagine the bustling world of mobile language learning apps. Standing out can feel like shouting in a crowded marketplace. A dynamic language learning app, brimming with interactive lessons and gamified learning experiences, faced this very challenge. Their existing mobile ad strategy, while functional, wasn't captivating enough to grab user attention within the crucial first few seconds. The result? Download rates stagnated, and brand awareness remained low. The app needed a fresh approach to mobile advertising, a strategy that would entice users, translate their interest into downloads, and solidify their position within the competitive language learning landscape.

Solution: Speaking the Language of Mobile Users: Design with Intent

The app's creators knew they needed to speak directly to their target audience: young professionals and students seeking a fun and effective way to learn a new language. They completely revamped their mobile ad strategy, focusing on three key areas:

- **Objective-Oriented Design:** The app's primary goal was clear: increase app downloads. Their new ads reflected this objective. Eye-catching visuals replaced generic stock photos. Instead, potential users were treated to snapshots of real-life scenarios – a young professional confidently ordering coffee in French, a student navigating public transportation in Spanish. These visuals showcased the practical application of the app, instantly sparking user interest.
- **Strategic Ad Formats:** The app's creators understood the power of variety. They experimented with different ad formats to cater to diverse user preferences:
    - **Carousel Ads:** These immersive ads functioned like mini-tours of the app. Each panel showcased a different aspect: a vibrant interface teeming with interactive lessons, gamified challenges that made learning fun, and even user testimonials praising the app's effectiveness. This multi-faceted approach allowed the app to pack a powerful punch within a single ad.
    - **Short Video Ads (Slideshow Format):** Capitalizing on the popularity of short-form video content, the app creators produced dynamic slideshow ads. These cost-effective gems were packed with engaging visuals

– think close-up shots of the intuitive app interface, interspersed with text overlays highlighting key features like bite-sized lessons and personalized learning pathways. The short format ensured they captured user attention without demanding a lengthy time commitment.
- **Mobile-First Mentality:** The app prioritized a seamless mobile experience. They ensured their ads were specifically formatted for various screen sizes, guaranteeing optimal viewing on any smartphone. Fast loading times were paramount, understanding that mobile users have little patience for sluggish content. The all-important "Download Now" button was prominently displayed, clear and easy to locate with a fingertip.

Results: From Applause to App Downloads: A Winning Strategy
The data spoke volumes:

- **Engagement Soared:** Within the first week of launching the new ad campaign, the app witnessed a 78% increase in average time spent viewing their mobile ads. Users were no longer just glancing; they were actively engaged with the content, a testament to the captivating visuals and informative messaging.
- **Downloads Spiked:** The most crucial metric – app downloads – skyrocketed by a remarkable 120%. The app's strategic use of mobile ad formats effectively translated user interest into action, propelling the app towards its download goals.
- **Brand Recognition Blossomed:** The consistent brand aesthetic applied across all ad formats – from color palettes to fonts – fostered brand recognition. The app was no longer just another anonymous app in the sea of mobile offerings; they were establishing itself as a trusted language-learning companion.

Key Takeaways:
- Choose ad formats that effectively showcase your app's functionalities and resonate with your target audience.
- Develop mobile ads that demonstrate the value proposition of your app in a clear, concise, and engaging manner.
- Optimize your ads for seamless mobile viewing, ensuring a positive user experience from the first impression.

Notes:
- Choose an ad format that aligns with your ad objective.
- Develop ads that effectively demonstrate the practical application of your product or service in a coherent and uniform manner.
- Optimize your ads to enhance the mobile user experience.

Optimize Meta Solutions

Introduction
To truly unlock the potential of your Meta campaigns, you need to optimize them for maximum impact. This section unveils the powerhouses within Meta Business Suite that propel your campaigns to peak performance. We'll dive into the Meta Pixel and Conversions API, explore website event tracking, and introduce the A/B testing feature.

Meta Pixel and the Conversions API
The Meta Pixel and Conversions API stand out as essential tools within the Meta Business suite, facilitating enhanced advertising efficiency by tracking customer interactions on business websites and gathering valuable customer data.

- The Meta Pixel, a compact code snippet, integrates seamlessly into business websites, refining ad performance measurement, ensuring precise results, and facilitating the creation of targeted audience segments.
- Leveraging the Meta Pixel, businesses can meticulously monitor specific customer actions and track metrics pertinent to their business objectives.
- Similarly, the Conversions API empowers advertisers by enabling the seamless transmission of customer data for precise targeting, optimization, and measurement of Facebook and Instagram ad campaigns. Combining the Conversions API with the Meta Pixel is advisable for businesses aiming to optimize campaign performance across Meta platforms.

Add the Meta Pixel to a Website
Adding the Meta Pixel to a website can be accomplished through various methods:

- **Connect with a partner platform:** Businesses collaborating with partners have the option to integrate the Meta Pixel seamlessly without the need to directly edit their website code. Partners also assist in streamlining ad creation, reporting, and evaluating user actions.
- **Manual installation:** For those preferring a hands-on approach, setting up the Meta Pixel independently involves copying and pasting the base code directly into the website's code.

How Does Conversions API Work?
The Conversions API is engineered to uphold data integrity and support advertisers' commitment to safeguarding user privacy. It offers enhanced data control when deployed independently from the Meta Pixel, facilitating a broader spectrum of data for informed advertising decisions and bolstered data exchange.

Advantages of the Conversions API
- **Improved Data Sharing Reliability:** Data transmission via the Conversions API tends to be more dependable compared to browser-based methods. Its design minimizes susceptibility to issues like browser crashes and connectivity disruptions.
- **Comprehensive Visibility Across the Funnel:** Advertisers leveraging the Conversions API gain access to a diverse range of data to inform their advertising strategies beyond what the Meta Pixel alone offers. This encompasses CRM data, lower-funnel events (such as qualified leads), and multi-site conversion pathways.

To optimize data sharing with Meta technologies, it's recommended to utilize both the Conversions API and the Meta Pixel concurrently. This ensures a more robust data connection, enabling advertisers to continuously deliver tailored experiences to users.

Standard and Custom Website Events
Events refer to activities occurring on your website, such as completing a purchase or adding an item to a cart. As users engage with your business, these events can be relayed to Meta technologies using integration methods like the Conversions API and the Meta Pixel. Two categories of events are recognized:

- **Standard Events:** These are actions acknowledged and supported by Meta technologies across various advertising products. Examples include Add Payment Info, Add to Cart, Add to Wishlist, Purchase, and Subscribe.
- **Custom Events:** These allow tracking of any website action not covered by standard events on Meta technologies, such as newsletter sign-ups. In cases where predefined standard events do not fit, businesses have the flexibility to create their own custom events.

Run A/B Tests
A/B tests enable the comparison of two versions of an ad to determine the more effective one. Here's how it works:

- Set up an A/B test within Ads Manager at the campaign, ad set, or ad level.
- Your audience is divided into subgroups, each exposed to a campaign, ad set, or ad differing by a single variable. These variables include ad creative, audience, placement, product sets, and ad delivery.
- A/B testing divides your budget equally and randomly allocates exposure between each version of your creative, audience, or placement. The performance of each strategy is then measured based on cost-per-result or cost-per-conversion lift.
- Upon completion of the test, you'll receive results on its performance. The most effective ad strategy will be identified under the "Winning ad was found" section. Additionally, you'll see results for each tested ad strategy, including metrics like cost per result, impressions, and spend.

Case Study: Metamorphosis for a Mega Retailer: How an E-commerce Giant Boosted Sales with Meta Business Suite Optimization

Challenge: Stalled Sales and Fragmented Data: E-commerce Giant Seeks Conversion Magic
A once-thriving e-commerce giant, facing a harsh reality – online sales were plateauing. Despite significant investment in advertising, campaign performance remained stagnant. The culprit? Inefficient targeting and a lack of clear data on user interactions with their website. They needed a solution to bridge the gap between ad exposure and conversions, a way to ensure their targeted ads were reaching the right people at the right time. They required a strategy that would not only optimize their return on ad spend (ROAS) but also unlock valuable customer insights to inform future marketing efforts.

Solution: Building a Data-Driven Bridge with Meta Business Suite
The e-commerce giant knew they needed to leverage the power of data to optimize their advertising efforts. They turned to Meta Business Suite, a comprehensive suite of tools designed to streamline Facebook and Instagram advertising campaigns. Here's how they harnessed the suite's potential:

- **Meta Pixel Magic:** The giant seamlessly integrated the Meta Pixel, a tiny code snippet, into their website. This seemingly insignificant addition acted as a game-changer. The Meta Pixel functioned like a silent observer, tracking critical customer interactions on their website. Product views, time spent browsing specific categories, even abandoned shopping carts – all this valuable data was meticulously collected by the Pixel. This real-time user

behavior data empowered them to create highly targeted audience segments based on specific actions and interests.
- **Conversions API: The Data Pipeline:** While the Meta Pixel provided valuable website behavior data, the giant yearned for a more robust connection between their ad campaigns and internal sales data. This is where the Conversions API came into play. The API acted as a secure data pipeline, establishing a direct link between their website's sales platform and Facebook and Instagram ad platforms. This two-way communication ensured seamless transmission of customer data, including critical post-conversion details like purchase value and specific items bought.
- **A/B Testing: The Refinement Engine:** The giant understood that the key to successful advertising lies in continuous optimization. They leveraged the A/B testing functionalities within Meta Business Suite to pit different ad variations against each other in a head-to-head battle for user attention and conversions. Imagine testing two versions of an ad for a new line of sportswear – one featuring a celebrity endorsement, the other showcasing real people enjoying active lifestyles. A/B testing allowed them to compare the performance of these ad variations across defined audience segments. By analyzing metrics like click-through rates, add-to-cart actions, and ultimately, purchases, the giant could identify the clear winner – the ad variant that resonated most effectively with their target audience.

Results: A Conversion Renaissance: E-commerce Giant Discovers Data-Driven Success

The implementation of Meta Business Suite tools yielded a dramatic transformation for the e-commerce giant:

- **Targeting Triumph:** By leveraging the combined power of the Meta Pixel and Conversions API, the giant achieved significantly enhanced targeting capabilities. Their ads were no longer scattered shots in the dark; they were laser-focused messages reaching highly relevant customer segments with a genuine interest in their products. This resulted in a remarkable **42% increase in click-through rates** on their Facebook and Instagram ads.
- **ROI Revolution:** A/B testing proved to be a goldmine for optimizing ad spend. By identifying high-performing ad creatives and audience segments, the giant was able to allocate their budget more effectively. This data-driven approach yielded a **28% reduction in cost-per-acquisition**, translating to more conversions for every dollar spent on advertising.
- **Streamlined Success:** Meta Business Suite provided the giant with a centralized platform to manage all aspects of its Facebook and Instagram advertising campaigns. The intuitive interface and automated reporting features streamlined the optimization process, allowing their marketing team to focus on strategic decision-making rather than manual data analysis.

Key Takeaways:
- Target smarter with Meta Pixel website behavior data.
- Optimize ad spend with Conversions API sales data link.
- Refine campaigns with A/B testing for top-performing ads.

Notes:
- The Meta Pixel functions as a small code snippet that can enhance outcomes, provide more precise measurement of results and facilitate the creation of new target audiences for ads on a business' website.
- The Conversions API establishes a direct link between your marketing data and various systems, enhancing ad targeting efficiency, reducing cost per action, and enabling result measurement across Meta technologies.
- Use A/B tests to analyze campaign variables like creative elements, audience targeting, ad placement, product sets, and delivery optimization, enabling informed decision-making for enhanced ad performance.

Reporting

Introduction
Meta Ads Manager empowers you to go beyond campaign creation. This section dives into the powerful reporting features, transforming raw data into actionable insights that fuel campaign success. By examining these reports, you'll gain a clear understanding of your campaign's effectiveness, identify winning strategies, and pinpoint areas for improvement – all crucial for optimizing future campaigns.

Meta Ads Manager
Analyzing the reports within Ads Manager provides insights into a business's progress toward achieving its advertising objectives. By examining the metrics, businesses can identify successful strategies and areas for improvement, which can guide future ad campaigns. Additionally, utilizing Ads Manager metrics allows for real-time optimization of ads during their active periods.

Default Metrics
In the Ads Manager interface, you have access to detailed insights at each level of your campaign: campaign, ad set, and ad. This allows you to assess the performance of both past and ongoing campaigns, ad sets, and ads using metrics tailored to your campaign objectives.

- **Campaigns Tab:** In this section, the dashboard is structured around individual ad campaigns. Here, you'll find a comprehensive overview of active and inactive campaigns, along with their respective performance metrics.
- **Ad Sets Tab:** In this segment, the dashboard is organized based on ad sets. You can filter the displayed ad sets by selecting a specific campaign from the Campaigns tab, streamlining your analysis to focus on particular campaigns.
- **Ads Tab:** Within this area, the dashboard provides insights on individual ads. Here, you can access information such as ad quality diagnostics, allowing for a detailed assessment of each advertisement's performance.

Results Metrics
Results metrics provide insights into the reach and effectiveness of an ad campaign.

- **Results:** This metric quantifies the instances where an ad successfully attains a desired outcome, aligning with the chosen objective and ad delivery optimization.
- **Reach:** This metric represents the total number of individuals who viewed the ads at least once. It differs from impressions, which may include multiple views of the same ads by a single person.
- **Impressions:** This metric gauges the frequency with which the ads appear on the screen for the specified audience.

Cost Metrics
Cost metrics provide insights into how the ad budget is utilized and its efficiency.

- **Cost Per Result:** This metric is derived by dividing the total expenditure by the number of achieved results. It indicates the campaign's cost-effectiveness in accomplishing its ad objectives.
- **Amount Spent:** This metric represents the estimated total expenditure on a campaign. For instance, it may show as $0.00 for a campaign under review or $6.57 for a recently approved and activated campaign. This figure should always be lower than the allocated budget.

To assess the effectiveness of a campaign, compare the predetermined metrics and goals with the campaign's actual results and cost metrics. Identify areas for enhancement within the campaign based on its outcomes, such as aligning business goals with ad objectives and optimizing budget allocation.

Other Ways to Review Performance

Understanding your audience is the cornerstone of successful social media marketing. This section empowers you to leverage the power of Facebook and Instagram Insights to gain valuable data about your followers and how they interact with your content.

Facebook Insights:
Facebook Insights offers a treasure trove of information about your Page's performance. Here's what you can uncover:

- **Audience Demographics:** Gain insights into the age, gender, and location of your followers, allowing you to tailor your content to resonate with their specific interests. (Note: Demographic data is available once you reach 100 followers.)
- **Content Performance:** Track how your posts are performing, including metrics like reach, engagement, and click-through rates. This data helps you understand what resonates with your audience and identify areas for improvement.
- **Important Note:** Facebook Insights only stores data for the past two years.

Instagram Insights:
While Instagram Insights doesn't offer demographic data, it provides valuable metrics for your organic and paid content. Here's how you can leverage these insights:

- **Post Performance:** Analyze engagement metrics like likes, comments, and shares for each post. This data helps you understand what content types resonate most with your audience.
- **Story Insights:** Track views, exits, and replies on your Stories to gauge their effectiveness in capturing attention.
- **Video and Reel Insights:** Analyze metrics like views, completion rates, and comments for your video and Reel content to understand what resonates with your audience in these formats.
- **Live Video Insights:** Gain insights into the number of viewers, peak viewers, and comments during your live streams.

Accessing Ad Insights: It's important to note that Instagram Insights on mobile devices primarily focus on organic content. To view insights for paid advertising campaigns, you'll need to access them through Ads Manager on a desktop computer.

Case Study: From Scattered Data to Soaring Sales: How a Digital Marketing Agency Cracked the Code on Meta Ads Reporting

Challenge: Drowning in Data, Starving for Insights
A digital marketing agency, facing rapid growth, found themselves struggling with a data deluge. Managing ad campaigns for diverse clients across various industries, they were overwhelmed with information. Metrics from Facebook Ads Manager poured in – impressions, clicks, conversions – but translating this data into actionable insights proved challenging. The core issue? A lack of a centralized reporting system. Without a clear view of campaign performance across different platforms (Facebook and Instagram), gauging success and optimizing campaigns for clients was an uphill battle. The agency needed a way to unify its data, identify winning strategies, and ultimately, drive significant results for its clients.

Reporting

Solution: Meta Ads Manager to the Rescue

The agency knew they needed a robust reporting solution to transform data into actionable insights. The answer came in the form of Meta Ads Manager's comprehensive reporting features. Here's how they harnessed this powerful tool:

- **Drilling Down for Details:** They moved beyond simply glancing at top-level campaign metrics. They leveraged the Campaigns, Ad Sets, and Ads tabs within Ads Manager to perform a deep dive. Imagine analyzing a Facebook ad campaign promoting a new line of athletic wear for a client. By drilling down to the Ad Sets level, the agency could assess the performance of different ad variations targeting specific demographics (young athletes) or interests (fitness enthusiasts). This granular analysis allowed them to identify which ad resonated most effectively with the target audience.
- **Metrics Mania: A Numbers Feast** The agency understood that success is a numbers game. They meticulously analyzed a range of default metrics within Ads Manager to gain a holistic view of campaign performance. Metrics like reach (number of unique users who saw the ad) and impressions (total number of times the ad was displayed) provided valuable insights into brand awareness. Results metrics, such as link clicks or website purchases driven by the ad, were crucial for gauging campaign effectiveness in achieving the client's goals (increased website traffic or e-commerce sales).
- **Cost Efficiency in Focus:** The agency didn't just focus on results; they were laser-focused on cost-effectiveness. Cost metrics like cost per click (CPC) and cost per acquisition (CPA) played a vital role. Imagine analyzing a client's Instagram ad campaign promoting a new cooking app. By keeping a close eye on the CPC, the agency could ensure they weren't paying an exorbitant price for each click on the ad. Similarly, monitoring CPA allowed them to track how much it costs to acquire a new app user through the campaign. This data-driven approach empowered them to optimize budgets and ensure maximum return on ad spend (ROAS) for their clients.
- **Beyond Ads Manager: Social Insights** The agency recognized the power of social listening. They strategically utilized Facebook and Instagram Insights to gather valuable data beyond just ad performance. Facebook Insights provided demographic breakdowns of the audience reached by the campaign, allowing the agency to refine its targeting for future campaigns. Instagram Insights offered a treasure trove of information on post-performance (engagement on organic content), Story insights (completion rates for client Stories), and video metrics (average view time).

Results: Data-Driven Decisions, Skyrocketing Sales

By leveraging Meta Ads Manager's reporting features and social media platform insights, the agency achieved significant results for their clients:

- **25% Increase in Click-Through Rates (CTRs):** Deeper analysis of ad performance at the Ad Set level allowed the agency to identify high-performing ad variations. By prioritizing these winning creatives, they achieved a significant increase in CTRs, driving more qualified traffic to their client's websites.
- **30% Reduction in Cost-Per-Acquisition (CPA):** Close monitoring of cost metrics like CPC and CPA empowered the agency to optimize ad spend and target the right audience more effectively. This resulted in a substantial reduction in CPA, translating to more conversions for every dollar spent on advertising.
- **Client Satisfaction Soars:** With data-driven insights guiding their decision-making, the agency was able to consistently deliver exceptional campaign performance for their clients. This resulted in a dramatic increase in client satisfaction and retention.

Key Takeaways:

- Dive deeper than top-level metrics by analyzing data at the Campaign, Ad Set, and Ad level in Meta Ads Manager.
- Analyze a range of metrics like reach, impressions, clicks, and cost-per-acquisition (CPA) to understand campaign effectiveness and optimize spend.

Reporting

- Leverage Facebook and Instagram Insights to gain audience demographics, content performance data, and user behavior to refine targeting and creatives.
- Monitor metrics like cost-per-click (CPC) to ensure efficient ad spend and maximize return on ad spend (ROAS) for clients.

Notes:
- Monitor various metrics and outcomes in Ads Manager at different levels—campaign, ad set, and ad—based on ad objectives and business goals.
- Evaluate the success of a campaign by comparing pre-launch metrics and goals with actual campaign results and cost metrics.
- Identify areas for improvement within a campaign, such as ensuring alignment of business goals with ad objectives and optimizing budget distribution.

Glossary

A/B Test: An A/B test is a controlled experiment comparing multiple ad sets to determine the best-performing option, often referred to as "split testing."

Ad: A piece of promotional content.

Ad Delivery: The process of specifying the maximum price you are willing to pay for a click, impression, or conversion.

Ad Format: The layout of an ad that dictates its appearance and the number of images or videos it contains.

Ad Level (Meta Ads Manager): In Ads Manager, the ad level is where individual ads are created as part of a campaign.

Ad Set: A group of ads that share the same daily or lifetime budget, schedule, bid type, bid information, and targeting criteria.

Ad Set Level (Ads Manager): In Ads Manager, the ad set level is where groups of ads are created within a campaign.

Meta Ads Manager: An interface where users can view, modify, and access performance reports for their campaigns, ad sets, and ads.

Ads Report: A report generated and managed in Ads Manager that showcases the performance of a set of ads.

Advantage+ Campaign Budget (Ads Manager): A setting in Ads Manager that allows Meta technologies to allocate your spend across ad sets for optimal overall performance.

Meta Audience Network: A network of approved mobile app publishers authorized by Meta to display ads in their apps.

Advantage+ Placements: An option selected when uploading ad content to Ads Manager that enables Meta technologies to automatically deliver ads on the most effective platforms.

Budget (Ads Manager): A setting in Ads Manager where you specify the maximum amount you are willing to spend on each ad set within a campaign.

Campaign: An advertisement or series of advertisements centered around a unified theme or attributes and targeted at a specific audience.

Campaign Level (Ads Manager): In Ads Manager, the campaign level is where you develop an advertisement or series of advertisements centered around a unified theme or attributes.

Campaign Objective: The desired outcome chosen by an advertiser to reflect their marketing goals, typically set at the initial stage of campaign creation in Ads Manager.

Carousel (Ad Format): Promotional content featuring multiple images or videos that can be scrolled horizontally.

Collections (Ad Format): Ad format that combines images and videos to enhance awareness and drive sales.

Conversions API: A direct channel used to collect customer activity data in a manner that respects users' data-sharing preferences on Meta platforms.

Glossary

Cost Per Action (CPA): Also referred to as "cost per acquisition," the expense incurred each time a specific action is taken as a result of an advertisement.

Cost Per Click (CPC): The price paid for each click on an advertisement.

Cost Per Impression (CPI): The expense associated with each view of an advertisement.

Cost Per Mille (CPM): Average cost or revenue generated for every 1,000 impressions of an advertisement.

Custom Audience: A group of individuals created using Meta's advertising tools, allowing advertisers to target existing audiences among Meta platform users.

Custom Event: An action logged based on specific user activity desired by the advertiser, such as actions on a website, app, or offline.

Data Source: A tool, connection, code snippet, or other entity utilized to gather information, such as the Meta Pixel, Facebook SDK, and offline conversions, for later analysis and measurement.

Event: A recorded action performed by individuals on your website, application, or offline, typically utilized for tracking and assessing the effectiveness of advertisements.

Instant Experience: A full-screen, post-click interaction that appears following a user's tap on a mobile advertisement.

Key Performance Indicator: A metric used to assess the effectiveness of a campaign or advertisement.

Lookalike Audience: A cohort of individuals who share similarities with an existing audience, enabling advertisers to target individuals who resemble their established customer base.

New Audiences: A default targeting option allowing advertisers to direct their advertisements towards individuals based on demographic, geographic, interest, and behavioral factors.

Meta Pixel: A small code snippet integrated into a website, facilitating access to Meta's most powerful advertising functionalities.

Placement: A specific area on a website or application where advertisements can be displayed, such as the feed, Instagram Stories, or Messenger Inbox.

Slideshow Ads: Advertisements that incorporate multiple images, text, and sound to capture attention and convey a narrative.

Targeting: The process of defining a specific audience for advertising purposes.

www.ingramcontent.com/pod-product-compliance
Lightning Source LLC
Chambersburg PA
CBHW062206220526
45470CB00009B/2936